THE TALE OF TWO FISHES

The Tale of Two Fishes is a therapeutic story about a journey to develop resilient thinking. A little girl feeds blue fishes with up-turned mouths and red fishes with down-turned mouths. The more she feeds the red fish, the bigger and more angry they become. The girl realises that if she feeds the blue fish and ignores the red, the blue fish will thrive. The story teaches children about the importance of balanced thinking and not dwelling too much on negative thoughts. This beautifully illustrated storybook will appeal to all children, and can be used by practitioners, educators and parents as a tool to discuss the importance of resilient thinking and the control we have over our own thoughts and behaviour.

Juliette Ttofa is a Specialist Senior Educational Psychologist with 15 years' experience working with children and young people. She specialises in supporting resilience and well-being in vulnerable children.

Julia Gallego is a picture book illustrator and designer, and a graduate of the Manchester School of Art.

For Sophia
X

First published 2018 by Routledge
2 Park Square, Milton Park, Abingdon, Oxon OX14 4RN

52 Vanderbilt Avenue, New York, NY 10017

Routledge is an imprint of the Taylor & Francis Group, an informa business

British Library Cataloguing-in-Publication Data
A catalogue record for this book is available from the British Library

Library of Congress Cataloging-in-Publication Data
A catalog record for this title has been requested

ISBN: 978-1-138-30884-8 (pbk)
ISBN: 978-1-315-14317-0 (ebk)

Typeset in Calibri
by Apex CoVantage, LLC

The Tale of Two Fishes

A Story About Resilient Thinking

Juliette Ttofa

Illustrated by Julia Gallego

Routledge
Taylor & Francis Group

LONDON AND NEW YORK

There were once two small fish who lived in a pond.
Each day a little girl would wander down to the pond to feed the fish.

One fish was red with a down-turned mouth and
the other was blue with an up-turned mouth.

Both fish were very hungry and would
often race each other
to see who could win
the most fish food.

After a few weeks, the little girl noticed that when she fed the red fish with the down-turned mouth, more red fish would come to be fed, until there were many, many red fish all gobbling up the food.

Some red fish were angry, some were worried, some were sad.

More and more red fish swarmed towards the food until the poor little blue fish with the up-turned mouth had nothing to feed on.

Weeks passed by and the same thing happened each time. As the girl fed the red fish, more and more shoals of them would come and wolf down the fish food until there was none left for the poor little blue fish.

Until the day came when the little blue fish with the up-turned mouth was nowhere to be seen.

And the big red fish with the down-turned mouths had grown bigger and redder and angrier until the whole of the pool blazed like a sea of fire!

Their down-turned mouths opened wide like gaping, rocky chasms.

Their teeth were suddenly as sharp as great spears.

Their eyes were as big as boulders.

And their tails were as giant as a whale's!

"This pond must be bottomless!" thought the little girl in a panic.

The little girl was also very sad. She missed the little blue fish with the up-turned mouth very much.

But the red fish grew more and more hungry until
the little girl could not satisfy their appetites.

They began to scramble up the banks of the pond like sea monsters – their giant
fins flailing to be free of the water.

"Get away! Get away!" the little girl shouted. But as much as
she tried to beat them back in anger, still more would come.

6

"How did this happen?" the little girl cried.

"How did the red fish grow so big and so many? How did they take over this pond?"

"Don't ask me!" a little voice replied. "You're the one who feeds them!"

Then the little girl looked down and noticed a snail going about his daily business.

"Don't worry," said the snail. "They won't survive long in the open air. They need food and water."

"The red fish come and the red fish go,
but feed them and they start to grow,"
sang the snail as he slid slowly away.

"I feed them?" answered the girl. "I feed them!" exclaimed the girl in delight.

"So I can stop feeding them! Maybe it would be better if I stopped feeding the red fish and only fed the blue fish."

No sooner had the words been uttered from her mouth than she noticed something small and blue shimmering in the distance. It was the little blue fish!

She went over and carefully began to feed the little blue fish again.

She noticed the big red fish trying to clamber up the bank behind her, but didn't pay them any attention.

Sure enough, the red fish shrank back into the depths of the pond.

And after a while the little blue fish grew nice and strong.

And as his smile grew, so did the little girl's,

and they became

best friends forever.